Our Daily Bread

Basics For Christian Living
Revised Edition

Publisher:	*RBC Ministries Asia Ltd*
Project Co-ordinators:	Lim Chien Chong, Sim KT
Editors:	Dean Ohlman, Esther Ho
Project Team:	Ong Chee Hong, Lai Mun Heng, Lu Mei Ying
	Wu Xiao Fen, Lee Min Sen, Lim Lian Sze
	Chen Mei Ling, Angela Aw, Koh Su Fen, Timothy Hia
Graphic Design Team:	Alex Soh, Janet Chim
Writers:	Haddon W. Robinson, David C. McCasland
	David C. Egner, Joanie E. Yoder, Richard W. De Haan
	J. David Branon, Vernon C. Grounds, Herbert Vanderlugt
	Martin R. De Haan II, Dennis J. De Haan, John Carvalho

With special thanks to Mart De Haan for his contribution in the development of this project.

RBC Ministries
RADIO BIBLE CLASS ~ FOUNDED 1938

A Guide For Your Journey

TOPIC:				
CHRISTIAN ASSURANCE	Discovery 1 Subtopic: Assurance Of Salvation 1 Jn 5:9-13 Title: More Than A Contract	Discovery 8 Subtopic: God's Grace 1 Cor 15:3-4, 8-11 Title: Our Image Problem	Discovery 15 Subtopic: Assurance Of Forgiveness 1 Jn 1:8-2:2 Title: All Is Forgiven	Discovery 22 Subtopic: God's Presence Ps 139:1-10 Title: From A Distance
CHRISTIAN LIVING	Discovery 2 Subtopic: Facing Persecution 2 Cor 4:16-18 Title: When You Are Hated	Discovery 9 Subtopic: Facing Temptation 1 Cor 10:11-13 Title: What's Your Load Limit?	Discovery 16 Subtopic: Facing Trials Gen 50:15-21 Title: On Purpose	Discovery 23 Subtopic: Being Thankful 1 Thess 5:16-18 Title: Count Your Blessings
CHRISTIAN SERVICE	Discovery 3 Subtopic: Serving Jn 13:12-17 Title: Tale Of A Towel	Discovery 10 Subtopic: Giving Lk 21:1-4 Title: The Widow's Millions	Discovery 17 Subtopic: Sacrifice Rom 12:1-8 Title: Do Your Own Thing	Discovery 24 Subtopic: Humility Mk 10:35-45 Title: King Of The Apes
KNOWING GOD	Discovery 4 Subtopic: Knowing The Bible Ps 19:7-11 Title: Spring Beauty	Discovery 11 Subtopic: God's Sovereignty Ps 121 Title: He's Up Anyway!	Discovery 18 Subtopic: Christ's Lordship Acts 22:4-10 Title: Two Crucial Questions	Discovery 25 Subtopic: Holy Spirit's Power Jn 16:7-15 Title: Lesson Of The 18-Wheeler
RELATING WITH GOD	Discovery 5 Subtopic: Faith 1 Sam 17:31-37 Title: E-mail Challenge	Discovery 12 Subtopic: Repentance 2 Cor 7:8-12 Title: Be Different!	Discovery 19 Subtopic: Worship Ps 95 Title: For Him	Discovery 26 Subtopic: Obedience 1 Sam 15:13, 7-11 Title: 100% Obedience
RELATING WITH NON-CHRISTIANS	Discovery 6 Subtopic: Love Not The World 1 Jn 2:15-17; Heb 12:1 Title: Weighed Down Or Way Up?	Discovery 13 Subtopic: Shine In The World Acts 8:1-8 Title: The Church In The World	Discovery 20 Subtopic: Praying For Them 1 Tim 2:1-8 Title: Prayer Evangelism	Discovery 27 Subtopic: Sharing With Them 1 Thess 1:5-8 Title: How Will They Hear?
RELATING WITH CHRISTIANS	Discovery 7 Subtopic: Church As A Body Rom 12:3-8 Title: Part Of A Whole	Discovery 14 Subtopic: Purpose Of Church Eph 4:11-13 Title: Use What You Have	Discovery 21 Subtopic: Church In Action Heb 10:19-25 Title: Grasshopper Christians	Discovery 28 Subtopic: Church In Unity Phil 2:1-11 Title: Others Or Me?

Welcome aboard! We're setting sail on an unforgettable journey through the Bible. Together, we're going to explore new seas and make some very exciting discoveries that will help you understand who God is while understanding what it takes to be a Christian. This expedition is certainly not for the faint-hearted! Ready for the adventure?

Let's weigh anchor and chart our path in the adventure of trusting and obeying Him!

Here's a map for the journey, which will help you get your bearings:

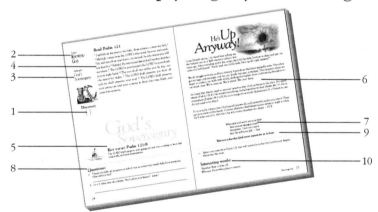

1. This number tells you how far you've gone in the 28 discoveries.

2. There are seven topics, and they tell you what aspect of Christian living we're dealing with in this study.

3. The subtopic tells you what aspect of the topic we are considering. A very handy clue.

4. The Bible passage is printed for your easy reference. Here, we use the New King James Version. Read this before you read the article on the right.

5. In case you are wondering which verse to focus on for the Bible passage, this will give you a headstart.

6. A brief story that brings the Bible truth to life. For maximum impact, read this after you've read the Scripture passage!

7. Bible truth in rhythm and rhyme.

8. The all-important questions. Don't skip this section if you can help it! It will help you think through God's truths and apply them in your life.

9. A catch phrase to help you remember what you have learned.

10. Gives you the meaning of words that may be unfamiliar to you.

Discovery

1

Read 1 John 5:9-13

⁹ If we receive the witness of men, the witness of God is greater; for this is the witness of God which He has testified of His Son. ¹⁰ He who believes in the Son of God has the witness in himself; he who does not believe God has made Him a liar, because he has not believed the testimony that God has given of His Son. ¹¹ And this is the testimony: that God has given us eternal life, and this life is in His Son. ¹² He who has the Son has life; he who does not have the Son of God does not have life. ¹³ These things I have written to you who believe in the name of the Son of God, that you may know that you have eternal life, and that you may continue to believe in the name of the Son of God.

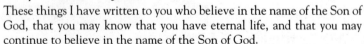

Key verse: 1 John 5:13

These things I have written to you who believe in the name of the Son of God, that you may know that you have eternal life, and that you may continue to believe in the name of the Son of God.

Questions:

a. Are there times when you are uncertain whether you are a child of God? What are some reasons that you feel this way?

_____

b. According to John, how does a person become a child of God and have eternal life? (See also John 1:12).

_____

More Than a Contract

We are all accustomed to contracts. We are often required to sign them, whether with a builder to construct our house or with the department store when we purchase an appliance. Contracts, formal or informal, write clearly what happens if one of the parties fails to live up to an agreement.

When we put our trust in Christ for salvation, however, we do more than sign a contract. We enter into a binding relationship with God whereby He makes us His children by the new birth and by adoption (1 Peter 1:23; Ephesians 1:5). Because of this close family relationship, we are permanent heirs of an eternal inheritance reserved in heaven for us (1 Peter 1:4).

Contracts can be broken if one of the parties fails to keep his part of the promise. Fortunately for us, our eternal destiny is based on more than some legal agreement we make with God. Rather, we are secure because of our family relationship with Him. If a youngster fails to show up for dinner, the parent's obligation isn't canceled. The parent starts a search for the child. One member's failure doesn't cancel the relationship.

How thankful we can be that eternal life is based on our relationship with God through Christ. —HWR

> We're members of God's family,
> We're children of the King;
> Because we've put our faith in Christ,
> To us He'll always cling. —Sper

We are heirs of God not merely by contract, but by birthright.

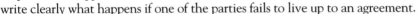

c. To help you know with certainty that you are truly a child of God, read "Can Anyone Know for Sure?". To order this booklet, please use Order Form on page 61.

Interesting words:

Testimony: Here, it means objective and authoritative evidence given by an eyewitness.
Eternal life: Personal relationship with God that will last forever.

Discovery

2

Read 2 Corinthians 4:16-18

[16] Therefore we do not lose heart. Even though our outward man is perishing, yet the inward man is being renewed day by day. [17] For our light affliction, which is but for a moment, is working for us a far more exceeding and eternal weight of glory, [18] while we do not look at the things which are seen, but at the things which are not seen. For the things which are seen are temporary, but the things which are not seen are eternal.

Facing Persecution

Key verse: 2 Corinthians 4:16

Therefore we do not lose heart. Even though our outward man is perishing, yet the inward man is being renewed day by day.

Questions:

a. Have other people ever discouraged or ridiculed you because of your belief in Jesus Christ? How did you respond?

_____

b. What does v.17 say about our afflictions?

_____

When *you* are Hated

As I was reading about Romanian believers who stood for Christ in the face of imprisonment, torture, and death, I thought of our Lord's exhortation, "And do not fear those who kill the body but cannot kill the soul. But rather fear Him who is able to destroy both soul and body in hell." (Matt 10:28)

All through church history, imprisoned and suffering Christians have found comfort in the assurance that God would deliver them—either back to their loved ones on earth or through death to the company of the saints already in heaven.

Although severe opposition to Christianity still exists in parts of the world, most of us don't face life-threatening persecution. But all Christians experience faith-testing trials.

Dennis Byrd, a former professional football player who is making an amazing recovery from a paralyzing injury, spoke of his faith in Christ on a secular talk show. But a caller vehemently denounced him for an earlier appearance on a Christian television program. The caller's hatred of Jesus Christ came through loud and clear.

Like believers down through the centuries, we can expect that we will be hated and attacked (John 15:18-19). But we need not be afraid. God is in control. We can say, "The Lord is on my side; I will not fear. What can man do to me?" —HVL

> *So send I you to hearts made hard by hatred,*
> *To eyes made blind because they will not see,*
> *To spend, though it be blood, to spend and spare not—*
> *So send I you to taste of Calvary.* —Clarkson

To be right with God may cause us to be in trouble with man.

---

c. If you are facing some problems at home, at the workplace or in school because of your faith in Jesus, you may want to talk to an older Christian about it.

Interesting words:

Perishing: Troubled and wearing out or dying.

Discovery

3

Read John 13:12-17

[12] So when He had washed their feet, taken His garments, and sat down again, He said to them, "Do you know what I have done to you? [13] You call me Teacher and Lord, and you say well, for so I am. [14] If I then, your Lord and Teacher, have washed your feet, you also ought to wash one another's feet. [15] For I have given you an example, that you should do as I have done to you. [16] Most assuredly, I say to you, a servant is not greater than his master; nor is he who is sent greater than he who sent him. [17] If you know these things, blessed are you if you do them."

Serving

Key verse: John 13:13-14

You call me Teacher and Lord, and you say well, for so I am. If I then, your Lord and Teacher, have washed your feet, you also ought to wash one another's feet.

Questions:

a. What do you think it means to serve God? Does it refer only to leaders and more mature Christians?

_____

b. Why shouldn't we feel that it is degrading or humiliating to serve others?

_____

Tale of a Towel

As a memento of a retreat I attended, I was given a small towel with a hand-stitched design symbolizing Jesus washing His disciples' feet. That towel served mostly as a decoration for a few years until one of my daughters accidentally used it to clean the car. The commemorative towel has been scrubbed with stain remover and sent through the washer, but it's indelibly marked by grease and grime.

At first I was miffed at having my memento used to wash hubcaps and bumpers. But then I began to see that towel as a picture of myself, and it caused me to ask some questions. When it comes to serving others, do I reserve myself for special occasions instead of doing an ordinary job today? When Jesus washed and wiped His disciples' feet, didn't His towel get dirty? What's a towel for—decoration or demonstration? Jesus said, "If I then, your Lord and Teacher, have washed your feet, you also ought to wash one another's feet." My little towel now serves as a reminder that self-preservation will keep me untouched but completely useless in my service for Christ. Real servants get dirty every day. —DCM

When Jesus washed His followers' feet,
He stooped to meet their need;
He showed us how to humbly serve,
To love in word and deed. —Sper

Decorations stay clean; disciples get dirty.

c. What act of service can you perform this week at home, in church, at the workplace or in school?

_____

Interesting words:

Teacher : A name of respect given to one who teaches God's laws.

Discovery

4

Read Psalm 19:7-11

[7] The law of the Lord is perfect, converting the soul; the testimony of the Lord is sure, making wise the simple; [8] The statutes of the Lord are right, rejoicing the heart; the commandment of the Lord is pure, enlightening the eyes; [9] The fear of the Lord is clean, enduring forever; the judgments of the Lord are true and righteous altogether. [10] More to be desired are they than gold, yea, than much fine gold; sweeter also than honey and the honeycomb. [11] Moreover by them Your servant is warned, and in keeping them there is great reward.

Knowing the Bible

Key verse: Psalm 19:10-11

More to be desired are they than gold, yea, than much fine gold; sweeter also than honey and the honeycomb. Moreover by them Your servant is warned, and in keeping them there is great reward.

Questions:

a. What were your first impressions of the Bible?

_____

b. The psalmist used some other words to refer to the Bible or God's Word. What are they?

_____

10

Spring Beauty

As we strolled through the woods together, my 9-year-old granddaughter taught me something about plants. I had scarcely noticed, until Kelsey pointed it out, that the forest floor was painted light pink with thousands of tiny flowers. "Those are spring beauties," she informed me. She went on to show me dogtooth violets, Dutchman's-breeches, and trillium.

After Kelsey called my attention to the wildflowers, I saw them everywhere. What a delicate beauty they brought to the landscape! And what interest and delight a young girl and her grandfather could share!

"If we come back in a week or so," I commented, "these flowers will be all gone. They're beautiful, but they last only a short time. We'll have to wait till next year to see them again." Kelsey already knew that. She had studied the seasons in school. What Kelsey didn't know is what wildflowers teach us about the Bible. The flowers last a few days and are gone, Isaiah told us, but the Word of God lasts forever (Isaiah 40:8). God's Word never fades, dries up, or blows away. Its treasures are there for us to appreciate each day.

Have you taken a walk through God's Word lately? Did you catch the beauty and majesty there? —DCE

The books men write are but a fragrance blown
From transient blossoms crushed by human hands;
But high above them all, splendid and alone,
Staunch as a tree, there is a Book that stands. —Frazee-Bower

The Bible—eternal truth and never-fading beauty.

c. Start a Bible reading program by reading a chapter of the Bible every day. You may want to start with the Gospel of John. This way you will finish reading the whole Bible in three years.

Interesting words:

Law: Here, it means teaching.
Testimony: Here, it refers to the entire law of God.
Statutes: What is mandated by God.

Topic:

RELATING WITH GOD

Subtopic:

Faith

Discovery

5

Read 1 Samuel 17:31-37

³¹ Now when the words which David spoke were heard, they reported them to Saul; and he sent for him. ³² Then David said to Saul, "Let no man's heart fail because of him; your servant will go and fight with this Philistine." ³³ And Saul said to David, "You are not able to go against this Philistine to fight with him; for you are a youth, and he a man of war from his youth." ³⁴ But David said to Saul, "Your servant used to keep his father's sheep, and when a lion or a bear came and took a lamb out of the flock, ³⁵ I went out after it and struck it, and delivered the lamb from its mouth; and when it arose against me, I caught it by its beard, and struck and killed it. ³⁶ Your servant has killed both lion and bear; and this uncircumcised Philistine will be like one of them, seeing he has defied the armies of the living God." ³⁷ Moreover David said, "The LORD, who delivered me from the paw of the lion and from the paw of the bear, He will deliver me from the hand of this Philistine." And Saul said to David, "Go, and the LORD be with you!"

Faith

Key verse: 1 Samuel 17:37

Moreover David said, "The LORD, who delivered me from the paw of the lion and from the paw of the bear, He will deliver me from the hand of this Philistine." And Saul said to David, "Go, and the LORD be with you!"

Questions:

a. Were there times when you felt really helpless and in need? Recall one such incident.

_____

b. Looking at David's example, what do you think "faith" is? (See also Hebrews 11:1).

_____

Challenge *E-mail*

It came to me as a two-sentence e-mail from Norway: "I think that God does not exist and I believe we are from monkeys! You are stupid to believe in God."

How do we respond to such a person? In his book *Foolishness to the Greeks*, Lesslie Newbigin suggests that we need to "hold and proclaim a belief that cannot be proven to be true" by the world's standards.

That's what David was doing when he said that with God's help he could defeat Goliath. He believed what could not be proven at that moment. He may have sounded foolish to the people around him, but he knew that the One he served would show Himself to be the true and living God.

In response to people who try to shake our faith, we can look at the example of David whom God has helped to defeat Goliath. We can affirm our confidence in the Bible's uncompromising truths. —DCE

God, give me the faith of a little child,
Who trusts so implicitly,
Who simply and gladly believes Thy Word
And never would question Thee. —Showerman

Faith sees things that are out of sight.

---

c. Is there a situation or a difficulty in your life now that requires you to exercise faith in God? How does this study help?

Interesting words:

Uncircumcised: In the Old Testament, if a male was uncircumcised, he was not one of God's chosen people and would not be able to enjoy God's blessings. Here, it means a person who does not believe in God.

RELATING WITH NON- CHRISTIANS

Subtopic:

Love not the World

Discovery

6

Read 1 John 2:15-17 & Hebrews 12:1

[15] Do not love the world or the things in the world. If anyone loves the world, the love of the Father is not in him. [16] For all that is in the world—the lust of the flesh, the lust of the eyes, and the pride of life—is not of the Father but is of the world. [17] And the world is passing away, and the lust of it; but he who does the will of God abides forever.

[1] Therefore we also, since we are surrounded by so great a cloud of witnesses, let us lay aside every weight, and the sin which so easily ensnares us, and let us run with endurance the race that is set before us.

Love not the world

Key verse: 1 John 2:15 -16

Do not love the world or the things in the world. If anyone loves the world, the love of the Father is not in him. For all that is in the world—the lust of the flesh, the lust of the eyes, and the pride of life—is not of the Father but is of the world.

Questions:

a. Make a list of some things you like to do that you know are not pleasing to God.

_____

b. What do the following phrases mean: "the lust of the flesh", "the lust of the eyes" and "the pride of life"?

_____

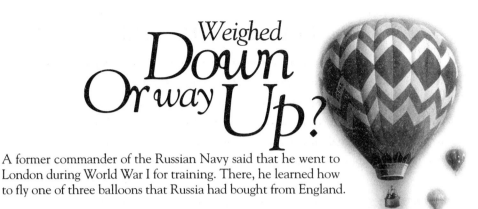

Weighed Down Or way Up?

A former commander of the Russian Navy said that he went to London during World War I for training. There, he learned how to fly one of three balloons that Russia had bought from England.

He recalled getting into the cabin and seeing all four sides covered with sandbags. To begin the ascent, sand was released until the huge balloon slowly lifted off the ground. As more sand went over the side, the craft ascended higher.

The man then applied this to our relationship with the Lord: "Now that I'm a Christian, I understand that when God begins to clean up my heart, He helps me to 'drop' these sins."

Hebrews 12:1 and 1 John 2:15 express that same spiritual truth. Carrying this world's weight restricts our relationship with the Lord and keeps our hearts from rising in love for Him. John wrote that we cannot love the world and love God at the same time. How often we have proven from experience just how true that is!

Selfish attitudes, besetting sins, and worldly cares keep us from "getting off the ground". But when we lay them aside, we experience the "uplifting" joy of a relationship with the Father. —MRD II

I want to live above the world,
Though Satan's darts at me are hurled;
For faith has caught the joyful sound,
The song of saints on higher ground. —Oatman

To go up, let go.

---

c. Look at the list you have made for the first question. Confess these things to God and ask Him to help you learn to "drop" them.

Interesting words:

World: Not the physical realm or the world of people, but the realm of evil and sin, which is controlled by the Devil.
Flesh: Body or sinful tendencies.

Discovery

7

Read Romans 12:3-8

³ For I say, through the grace given to me, to everyone who is among you, not to think of himself more highly than he ought to think, but to think soberly, as God has dealt to each one a measure of faith. ⁴ For as we have many members in one body, but all the members do not have the same function, ⁵ so we, being many, are one body in Christ, and individually members of one another. ⁶ Having then gifts differing according to the grace that is given to us, let us use them: if prophecy, let us prophesy in proportion to our faith; ⁷ or ministry, let us use it in our ministering; he who teaches, in teaching; ⁸ he who exhorts, in exhortation; he who gives, with liberality; he who leads, with diligence; he who shows mercy, with cheerfulness.

Church as a Body

Key verse: Romans 12:5

So we, being many, are one body in Christ, and individually members of one another.

Questions:

a. What do you think are some of your strengths?

_____

b. What do you think your spiritual gift(s) is/are? (See also 1 Corinthians 12:4-11)

_____

Part of a Whole

Twice in my life I've broken one of my little toes by colliding with furniture. Ouch! For days I limped painfully, my body protecting its tiny injured member. My body was doing exactly what it was designed to do. It supported and sympathized with the part of me that was hurting. Gradually my toe healed, resuming its thankless task.

Although I'll never again take my toes for granted, I sometimes take for granted certain members of the church. Paul taught that the church is the body of Christ (Romans 12:5), not merely like the body of Christ. Each member has God-given abilities (Romans 12:6a) to support and sympathize with other members.

If Christ's church is to function the way God designed it to, there are three things we dare not do: (1) Refuse to fellowship (share in common) with others. (2) Let fear and lack of love cause us to withhold our gifts from others. (3) Think lightly of others' gifts or disagree to let others use their gifts through pride and envy.

Instead, we need to be actively using our spiritual gifts to the benefit of fellow members of Christ's body. For each member belongs to all the other members (Romans 12:5) and so our God-given abilities are meant to be used for others as well.

God has placed us where we are, to use us according to the gifts He has given to us. We are members of the body of Christ. We are part of the whole. So let us do our part for the whole. —JEY

> We're all dependent on the strength
> *We draw from one another,*
> *For we're connected by the love*
> *That comes from God our Father.* —Sper

Each member of Christ's body must do its part.

---

c. How can you use your spiritual gift(s) to help another Christian?

Interesting words:

Gifts: Talents and special abilities given by God for the purpose of serving others.
Grace: Kindness and favour to someone who does not deserve it.

Discovery

8

Read 1 Corinthians 15:3-4, 8-11

³ For I delivered to you first of all that which I also received: that Christ died for our sins according to the Scriptures, ⁴ and that He was buried, and that He rose again the third day according to the Scriptures.

⁸ Then last of all He was seen by me also, as by one born out of due time. ⁹ For I am the least of the apostles, who am not worthy to be called an apostle, because I persecuted the church of God. ¹⁰ But by the grace of God I am what I am, and His grace toward me was not in vain; but I labored more abundantly than they all, yet not I, but the grace of God which was with me. ¹¹ Therefore, whether it was I or they, so we preach and so you believed.

Key verse: 1 Corinthians 15:10

But by the grace of God I am what I am, and His grace toward me was not in vain; but I labored more abundantly than they all, yet not I, but the grace of God which was with me.

Questions:

a. Have you ever felt that God could not possibly accept you as you are? Why did you feel this way? On the other hand, have you thought yourself better than others? Why did you feel you are better?

b. Consult a more mature Christian or a Bible dictionary on the meaning of the "grace of God".

Our Image problem

People who clearly understand their own strengths and weaknesses are better able to accept themselves as they are and accomplish more in life. They can identify with the person who said, "I'm only someone, but I am someone. I can't do everything, but I can do something."

The apostle Paul recognized his debts towards God, but he took his God-given assets and used them for eternal profit. His self-acceptance was based on God's acceptance of him in Christ. God's grace enabled him to affirm his apostleship while living with the painful memory of persecuting the church (1 Corinthians 15:9; 1 Timothy 1:13-15).

Paul didn't have a bad self-image when he called himself the "least of the apostles," nor was it false humility that prompted him to say he was "not worthy to be called an apostle" (1 Corinthians 15:9). Neither was it undue pride when he affirmed that he "labored more abundantly" than all of the other apostles (v.10). He was simply recognizing his human weaknesses while praising the effectiveness of God's grace. He knew he was able to serve God because he had been forgiven.

Trusting Jesus as Savior and Lord and being honest with ourselves will enable us to say, "By the grace of God I am what I am." That's a mature kind of self-acceptance. —DJD

> We all have faults uniquely ours,
> *Those flaws that cause self-blame,*
> *But God accepts us as we are,*
> *And we must do the same.* —DJD

**Our value is not in what we do for God
but in what Christ has done for us.**

---

c. How does knowing about God's grace change or influence the way you think of yourself and the way you relate to others?

Interesting words:

Persecuted: Hated and ill-treated (in this case, due to their faith in Jesus).

Apostles: Here, it refers to people who saw the risen Christ and who were specially commissioned by Him to be messengers of the Gospel.

Topic:

CHRISTIAN
LIVING

Subtopic:

*Facing
Temptation*

Discovery

9

Read 1 Corinthians 10:11-13

[11] Now all these things happened to them as examples, and they were written for our admonition, on whom the ends of the ages have come. [12] Therefore let him who thinks he stands take heed lest he fall. [13] No temptation has overtaken you except such as is common to man; but God is faithful, who will not allow you to be tempted beyond what you are able, but with the temptation will also make the way of escape, that you may be able to bear it.

*Facing
Temptation*

Key verse: 1 Corinthians 10:13

No temptation has overtaken you except such as is common to man; but God is faithful, who will not allow you to be tempted beyond what you are able, but with the temptation will also make the way of escape, that you may be able to bear it.

Questions:

a. What are some temptations you have faced? Which of these have you given in to and why?

_____

b. In v.13, what are the two things that God does for you when you are tempted?

_____

What is your *Load limit?*

We've all seen load-limit signs on highways, bridges, and elevators. Knowing that too much strain can cause severe damage or complete collapse, engineers determine the exact amount of stress various materials and manufactured items can safely endure. Posted warnings tell us not to exceed the maximum load.

Human beings also have their load limits, which vary from person to person. Some people, for example, can bear the pressure of trial and temptation better than others; yet everyone has a breaking point and can take only so much.

At times, circumstances and people seem to be pushing us beyond what we can bear. But the Lord knows our limitations and never allows any difficulties to enter our lives that exceed our strength and ability to endure. This is especially true when we're tempted by sin. According to 1 Corinthians 10:13, "No temptation has overtaken you except such as is common to man; but God is faithful, who will not allow you to be tempted beyond what you are able, but with the temptation will also make the way of escape, that you may be able to bear it."

So when trials and temptations press down on you, take courage! Remember, your heavenly Father knows the limits of your ability to stand up under life's pressures. Draw upon His strength. No temptation will ever be greater than that! —RWD

> When sorrows assail us or terrors draw nigh,
> *His love will not fail us, He'll guide with His eye;*
> *And when we are fainting and ready to fail,*
> *He'll give what is lacking and make us prevail.* —Anon.

If you give in to God, you won't cave in to sin.

c. To learn how to overcome sexual temptations, read "How Can I Resist The Lure of Sexual Sin?" To order this booklet, please use Order Form on page 61.

Interesting words:

Admonition: Reproof or encouragement that leads to correct behavior.
Temptation: Difficult experiences that prove our faith and help us grow. Or desires and attractions that can cause us to sin against God.

Discovery

10

Read Luke 21:1-4

¹ And He looked up and saw the rich putting their gifts into the treasury, ² and He saw also a certain poor widow putting in two mites. ³ So He said, "Truly I say to you that this poor widow has put in more than all; ⁴ for all these out of their abundance have put in offerings for God, but she out of her poverty put in all the livelihood that she had."

Key verse: Luke 21:3-4

So He said, "Truly I say to you that this poor widow has put in more than all; for all these out of their abundance have put in offerings for God, but she out of her poverty put in all the livelihood that she had."

Questions:

a. Why do you think people put money in the offering bag in church? What do you think the money is used for?

_____

b. Why did Jesus say (v.3) that the widow had put in more than all the others when in fact she had only put in two small copper coins?

_____

The Widow's Millions

Someone has calculated that if the widow's 2 mites had been deposited in a bank at 4-percent interest compounded semiannually, by today it would have grown to the sum of $4.8 billion trillion. What potential there is in such a small investment when it's left to grow for a long time!

In a more significant sense, that widow's 2-mite investment continues to reproduce itself to this very day. Only eternity will reveal how many of God's people have been challenged by that woman's sacrifice, and have dared to follow her example.

With some, it may have been a commitment to greater stewardship of their money. With others, it may have been the giving of themselves and their talents in service to Christ and His kingdom. How can we begin to estimate the eternal value of all the good that such self-giving service has produced down through the centuries? Like the widow, the poorest and least-talented Christians can invest in eternity when what they give represents sacrifice, devotion, and love for Christ.

Let's not underestimate the potential our small contributions can make to the cause of Christ. Only in eternity will this world's true millionaires be revealed. Will we be among them? —DJD

> If you cannot give a million,
> *You can give the widow's mite,*
> *And the least you do for Jesus*
> *Will be precious in His sight.* —Anon.

**The motive of the giver is more important
than the measure of the gift.**

c. Now that you have learned that the widow gave even though she was very poor, how much would you be able to give regularly for the Lord's work?

_____

Interesting words:

Treasury: Thirteen trumpet-shaped boxes for receiving the donations of worshippers.

Discovery

11

Read Psalm 121

[1] I will lift up my eyes to the hills - from whence comes my help? [2] My help comes from the LORD, who made heaven and earth. [3] He will not allow your foot to be moved; he who keeps you will not slumber. [4] Behold, He who keeps Israel shall neither slumber nor sleep. [5] The LORD is your keeper; the LORD is your shade at your right hand. [6] The sun shall not strike you by day, nor the moon by night. [7] The LORD shall preserve you from all evil; he shall preserve your soul. [8] The LORD shall preserve your going out and your coming in from this time forth, and even forevermore.

God's Sovereignty

Key verse: Psalm 121:8

The LORD shall preserve your going out and your coming in from this time forth, and even forevermore.

Questions:

a. Think of a difficult situation in which you received very timely help from someone. How did you feel?

_____

b. In v.5, what does the phrase, "the Lord is your keeper" mean?

_____

He's Up Anyway!

Linus Mandy wrote, "A friend was telling me she helped out at a kid's summer camp a few years ago. After rounding up for the camp, she told the kids, 'Let's go to sleep and put our cares in God's hands.' 'Yeah,' said one of the kids, 'He's up all night anyway!'"

We all struggle with the problem of worry. Fears about the future gradually arise. Then they get stronger and stronger, and we can finally become powerless. This happens when we begin to replace our faith with worry, shifting the burden from God's strong shoulders to our weak ones. We're anxious. We're afraid. We can't sleep.

At times like this we need to remind ourselves that God is always on the alert. He never sleeps (Psalm 121:4). He knows everything, including what we fear (Psalm 44:21). He is everywhere (Psalm 139:7-10). He is in charge of our world (Ephesians 1:11). Therefore, we do not need to be afraid.

Do you really believe that God sees all, knows all, is all-powerful, and is in control? Then put your cares in His hands. Commit whatever that's keeping you awake at night to Him. He'll take care of it. He's the One who never slumbers nor sleeps. —DCE

> When fear and worry test your faith
> *And anxious thoughts assail,*
> *Remember, God is in control*
> *And He will never fail.* —Sper

Worry is a burden God never meant for us to bear.

---

c. Select one verse from Psalm 121 that will remind you that the Lord is your keeper. Memorize the verse.

Interesting words:

Slumber: Rest or doze off.
Whence: From what place or source.

Discovery

12

Read 2 Corinthians 7:8-12

[8] For even if I made you sorry with my letter, I do not regret it; though I did regret it. For I perceive that the same epistle made you sorry, though only for a while. [9] Now I rejoice, not that you were made sorry, but that your sorrow led to repentance. For you were made sorry in a godly manner, that you might suffer loss from us in nothing. [10] For godly sorrow produces repentance leading to salvation, not to be regretted; but the sorrow of the world produces death. [11] For observe this very thing, that you sorrowed in a godly manner: what diligence it produced in you, what clearing of yourselves, what indignation, what fear, what vehement desire, what zeal, what vindication! In all things you proved yourselves to be clear in this matter. [12] Therefore, although I wrote to you, I did not do it for the sake of him who had done the wrong, nor for the sake of him who suffered wrong, but that our care for you in the sight of God might appear to you.

Repentance

Key verse: 2 Corinthians 7:10

For godly sorrow produces repentance leading to salvation, not to be regretted; but the sorrow of the world produces death.

Questions:

a. Recall an instance in which you knew you had sinned. Were you more sorry about the consequences (e.g. being rebuked or punished by others) or the fact that you had sinned against God? Did your attitude or behavior change after that incident?

b. What do you think Paul means when he says "godly sorrow produces repentance leading to salvation" (v.10)?

"Be different!"

Lloyd Ogilvie, the chaplain of the US Senate, tells about a time when he was having lunch with a prominent businessman. A woman, who recognized the executive, walked over to their table and greeted him with a hefty slap on his back, causing him to spill coffee on his suit. Then with a flamboyant gesture, she tossed her fur stole over her shoulder, brushing Dr. Ogilvie full in the face. "Oh, I'm so sorry," she apologized. The executive looked her straight in the eye and said, "Ma'am, don't be sorry, be different!"

When we sin, the Lord isn't interested in just a quick apology. He looks for a different attitude and a change of behavior. Scripture calls this godly sorrow that leads to repentance (2 Corinthians 7:9-10). Paul saw this sorrow in the Corinthian believers, which resulted from their response to an earlier letter of rebuke he had written (1 Corinthians 5:1-8). At first it bothered him that he had made them sorrowful (2 Corinthians 7:8), but when their sorrow led to a genuine change of heart, the apostle rejoiced (2 Corinthians 7:9-11).

Sorrow for sin can be good or bad. But when it leads to an intention to change, it brings freedom from guilt and the renewed joy of our salvation. —DJD

> Dear Lord, be merciful to us;
> *Our sin has grieved Your heart;*
> *And strengthen our resolve, O Lord,*
> *To make a fresh, new start.* —DJD

Repentance says, "I'm sorry," but also shows, "I'm through."

c. Pray and ask God to forgive you and help you repent of a specific sin.

Interesting words:

Repentance: Turning away from what is wrong and turning to God.
Indignation: Strong anger.
Vehement: With strong feeling, fervent.
Vindication: To be cleared of blame.

Read Acts 8:1-8

[1] Now Saul was consenting to his death. At that time a great persecution arose against the church which was at Jerusalem; and they were all scattered throughout the regions of Judea and Samaria, except the apostles. [2] And devout men carried Stephen to his burial, and made great lamentation over him. [3] As for Saul, he made havoc of the church, entering every house, and dragging off men and women, committing them to prison. [4] Therefore those who were scattered went everywhere preaching the word. [5] Then Philip went down to the city of Samaria and preached Christ to them. [6] And the multitudes with one accord heeded the things spoken by Philip, hearing and seeing the miracles which he did. [7] For unclean spirits, crying with a loud voice, came out of many who were possessed; and many who were paralyzed and lame were healed. [8] And there was great joy in that city.

Shine in the World

Key verse: Acts 8:4

Therefore those who were scattered went everywhere preaching the word.

Questions:

a. Being among the few Christians in school, at the workplace or at home, what do you do when family and friends pressure you to do things that are displeasing to God?

_____

b. What was one positive outcome of the persecution that has come upon the early church (vv.4-5)?

_____

The Church in the World

I recently saw a photograph of people leaving a church after a service. They were carrying Bibles and smiling. As I looked at those men, women, and children, I thought, there goes the church. The building will stay, and it will be referred to as "a church." But those bricks can't preach and those pews can't witness. Only people can do that.

Author R. C. Sproul wrote, "Where the people of God are, there is the church—under the lordship of Christ and indwelt by the Spirit."

This is the essence of the commission Jesus gave to His disciples just before He left them. He promised them power from the Holy Spirit, and said they would be His witnesses in Jerusalem, Judea, Samaria, and to the end of the earth (Acts 1:8). And when the first-century church of Jerusalem came under persecution, that's what happened. They were scattered and proclaimed the gospel wherever they went (Acts 8:4).

When believers in Jesus Christ leave a worship service, the building stays, but God's people —the church—fan out into the community. Throughout the week, they continue to be the church wherever they are in the world—in shops, schools, restaurants, and homes. I wonder, is the world hearing the gospel from the church? —DCE

The witness of the church on earth
Must shine with brightest light;
To all who need the second birth
And strength to live aright. —JDB

The world won't go to the church, so the church must go to the world.

c. To learn how to share the Gospel with a friend, read "How Can I Break the Silence?" To order this booklet, please use Order Form on page 61.

Interesting words:

Apostles: See meaning on page 19.
Lamentation: Mourning.

Topic:

RELATING
WITH
CHRISTIANS

Subtopic:

*Purpose of
the Church*

Read Ephesians 4:11-13

[11] And He Himself gave some to be apostles, some prophets, some evangelists, and some pastors and teachers, [12] for the equipping of the saints for the work of ministry, for the edifying of the body of Christ, [13] till we all come to the unity of the faith and of the knowledge of the Son of God, to a perfect man, to the measure of the stature of the fullness of Christ.

Discovery

14

Key verse: Ephesians 4:11-12

And He Himself gave some to be apostles, some prophets, some evangelists, and some pastors and teachers, for the equipping of the saints for the work of ministry, for the edifying of the body of Christ.

Questions:

a. What do you think of when people mention the word "church"?

_____

b. What does Paul say God is preparing believers for?
    In the light of that, what kind of attitude should we have towards the church?

_____

Use what you have

A group of animals decided to improve their general welfare by starting a school. The curriculum included swimming, running, climbing, and flying. The duck, an excellent swimmer, was deficient in other areas, so he majored in climbing and flying, much to the detriment of his swimming. The rabbit, a superior runner, was forced to spend so much time in other classes that he soon lost much of his famed speed. The squirrel, who had been rated "A" as a climber, dropped to a "C" because his instructors spent hours trying to teach him to fly. And the eagle could no longer soar to the treetops because he had to learn how to swim.

What happened to this group of animals portrays what often occurs in our churches. Ephesians 4:11-13 teaches that we are all given certain gifts. But some of us serve in so many areas that our tasks are not done well. As a result, the whole church suffers.

If God made you a teacher, be a teacher. Study diligently and do your best. If He's given you the gift of mercy, serve cheerfully and don't expect others to do what you do. Accept your spiritual gifts. Cultivate your capabilities. Stop comparing. Enjoy being you.

Yes, use what you have! —RWD

> *Be not always wanting*
> *Some other work to do,*
> *But cheerfully perform the task*
> *That Christ has given you.* —Anon.

Do what you can, where you are, with what you have. —Moody

---

c. Explore with a more mature Christian something you can do to serve the church and how to go about doing it.

Interesting words:

Equipping of the saints: Preparing and training believers.
Edifying: Building for spiritual growth and maturity.

Discovery

15

Read 1 John 1:8 - 2:2

⁸ If we say that we have no sin, we deceive ourselves, and the truth is not in us. ⁹ If we confess our sins, He is faithful and just to forgive us our sins and to cleanse us from all unrighteousness. ¹⁰ If we say that we have not sinned, we make Him a liar, and His word is not in us.

¹ My little children, these things I write to you, so that you may not sin. And if anyone sins, we have an Advocate with the Father, Jesus Christ the righteous. ² And He Himself is the propitiation for our sins, and not for ours only but also for the whole world.

Assurance of Forgiveness

Key verse: 1 John 1:9

If we confess our sins, He is faithful and just to forgive us our sins and to cleanse us from all unrighteousness.

Questions:

a. Do you have difficulty believing that God forgives all your sins? Why do you feel this way?

_____

b. What aspects of God's character tell you that God will definitely forgive and cleanse you when you confess your sins? (1 John 1:9)

_____

All is forgiven

A woman who was extremely upset phoned me several years ago. She said she was on the verge of a nervous breakdown. Apparently she had strayed far from the Lord, but now had returned to Him and truly wanted to do His will. The memories of her days of spiritual wandering, however, kept haunting her. She somehow couldn't accept the fact that God had forgiven her sins, and she had no peace or joy. But worse than that, by her attitude she was saying to God, "I don't believe you. You don't mean what you say!"

I said to her, "Suppose that one of your dearest friends was careless and broke a piece of your best china. Feeling very sorry, she sincerely apologized for not being more careful. You assured her that you would not hold it against her. Now, what would you think if every time you saw that person, she recalled how foolish she had been and again asked for forgiveness? After a while you would probably become exasperated and say, 'Listen, put the matter out of your mind. I have sincerely forgiven you, and I don't want you to mention it again!' "

God is also true to His Word, for He promises to cleanse us when we acknowledge our failures. So confess your sins to the Lord. Then believe that you're forgiven. —RWD

In the deep, silent depths, far away from the shore
Where they never may rise to trouble me more—
God has buried my sins where no mortal may see;
He has cast all of them in the depths of the sea. —Anon.

Having given your sins to God, don't try to take them back.

---

c. Instead of focusing on your guilt and mistakes, what can you do in future to remind yourself of God's promise? ❏ memorize 1 John 1:9
❏ use this verse as a prayer to God

Interesting words:

Unrighteousness: Unholy living that does not meet God's standards.
Propitiation: Christ satisfied and appeased God's anger by taking the punishment for sin on our behalf.

CHRISTIAN LIVING

Subtopic:

Facing Trials

Discovery

16

Read Genesis 50:15-21

¹⁵ When Joseph's brothers saw that their father was dead, they said, "Perhaps Joseph will hate us, and may actually repay us for all the evil which we did to him." ¹⁶ So they sent messengers to Joseph, saying, "Before your father died he commanded, saying, ¹⁷ 'Thus you shall say to Joseph: "I beg you, please forgive the trespass of your brothers and their sin; for they did evil to you."' Now, please, forgive the trespass of the servants of the God of your father." And Joseph wept when they spoke to him. ¹⁸ Then his brothers also went and fell down before his face, and they said, "Behold, we are your servants." ¹⁹ Joseph said to them, "Do not be afraid, for am I in the place of God? ²⁰ But as for you, you meant evil against me; but God meant it for good, in order to bring it about as it is this day, to save many people alive. ²¹ Now therefore, do not be afraid; I will provide for you and your little ones." And he comforted them and spoke kindly to them.

Facing Trials

Key verse: Genesis 50:20

But as for you, you meant evil against me; but God meant it for good, in order to bring it about as it is this day, to save many people alive.

Questions:

a. Being a Christian means sometimes having to go through trials. Why do you think this is necessary and how do you feel about this?

_____

b. What do you think Genesis 50:20 and Romans 8:28 have in common?

_____

On Purpose

When a cowboy applied for an insurance policy, the agent asked, "Have you ever had any accidents?" After a moment's reflection, the applicant responded, "Nope, but a horse did kick in two of my ribs last summer, and a couple of years ago a rattlesnake bit me on the ankle."

"Wouldn't you call those accidents?" replied the puzzled agent. "No," the cowboy said, "They did it on purpose!"

That story reminds me of the biblical truth that there are no accidents in the lives of God's children. In today's Scripture, we read how Joseph interpreted a difficult experience that had seemed like a great calamity. He had been thrown into a pit and then sold as a slave. This was a great test of his faith, and from the human standpoint it appeared to be a tragic case of injustice, not a providential means of blessing. But Joseph later learned that "God meant it for good" (Genesis 50:20).

Are you passing through the deep waters of trial and disappointment? Does everything seem to be going against you? These apparent misfortunes are not accidents. The Lord allows such things for a blessed purpose. So, patiently trust Him. If you know the Lord, someday you will praise Him for it all! —RWD

What looks like just an accident
When viewed through human eyes,
Is really God at work in us—
His blessing in disguise. —Sper

God transforms trials into triumphs.

---

c. To have a better understanding of the value of suffering in the life of a Christian, read "Why Would a Good God Allow Suffering?" To order this booklet, please use Order Form on page 61.

Interesting words:

Trespass: Here, it means treacherous acts or wickedness toward another.

Discovery

17

Read Romans 12:1-8

[1] I beseech you therefore, brethren, by the mercies of God, that you present your bodies a living sacrifice, holy, acceptable to God, which is your reasonable service. [2] And do not be conformed to this world, but be transformed by the renewing of your mind, that you may prove what is that good and acceptable and perfect will of God. [3] For I say, through the grace given to me, to everyone who is among you, not to think of himself more highly than he ought to think, but to think soberly, as God has dealt to each one a measure of faith. [4] For as we have many members in one body, but all the members do not have the same function, [5] so we, being many, are one body in Christ, and individually members of one another. [6] Having then gifts differing according to the grace that is given to us, let us use them: if prophecy, let us prophesy in proportion to our faith; [7] or ministry, let us use it in our ministering; he who teaches, in teaching; [8] he who exhorts, in exhortation; he who gives, with liberality; he who leads, with diligence; he who shows mercy, with cheerfulness.

Sacrifice

Key verse: Romans 12:1

I beseech you therefore, brethren, by the mercies of God, that you present your bodies a living sacrifice, holy, acceptable to God, which is your reasonable service.

Questions:

a. Sacrifice entails giving up things that are dear to us. What are some sacrifices you have made as a result of obeying Christ?

_____

b. Why do you think the Bible tells us to "present our bodies a living sacrifice" (v.1)? You may want to refer to a Bible commentary for help.

_____

Do your Own thing

In the 60s and 70s, much was heard about the right of individuals to "do their own thing." People were encouraged to be themselves, to get to know themselves, and to express themselves.

Of course a Christian should never pursue an unhealthy individualism that glorifies self and ignores God. But when we remember our responsibility to others and acknowledge our dependence on the Lord, He can use our distinctive skills and spiritual gifts for His glory.

In Romans 12, believers are reminded that while they are part of one body, they all have different God-given abilities. Every child of God is obligated to recognize his particular talents and to use them in His service.

In a commercial airliner, the pilot, co-pilot, mechanics, engineers, and flight attendants all have different responsibilities. What jeopardy the passengers would be in if each crew-member neglected his duties for another role! In much the same way, serious harm can come to a church if its members clamor for the position of another.

Don't settle for less than God's best by coveting a position you may not be suited for. Recognize the gift God has given you and "do your own thing." And do it well! —RWD

It matters not what others do;
It is my task to see
My life is patterned to the mold
The Lord has planned for me. —Anon.

Your place is where you can do the most good for God.

c. In view of vv. 7-8, what is one area in which you can serve Him more?

Interesting words:

Sacrifice: Committing every area of one's life to God.

Discovery

18

Read Acts 22:4-10

⁴ "I persecuted this Way to the death, binding and delivering into prisons both men and women, ⁵ as also the high priest bears me witness, and all the council of the elders, from whom I also received letters to the brethren, and went to Damascus to bring in chains even those who were there to Jerusalem to be punished. ⁶ Now it happened, as I journeyed and came near Damascus at about noon, suddenly a great light from heaven shone around me. ⁷ And I fell to the ground, and heard a voice saying to me, 'Saul, Saul, why are you persecuting Me?' ⁸ So I answered, 'Who are You, Lord?' And He said to me, 'I am Jesus of Nazareth, whom you are persecuting.' ⁹ And those who were with me indeed saw the light and were afraid, but they did not hear the voice of Him who spoke to me. ¹⁰ So I said, 'What shall I do, Lord?' And the Lord said to me, 'Arise and go into Damascus, and there you will be told all things which are appointed for you to do.'"

Christ's Lordship

Key verse: Acts 22:10

So I said, 'What shall I do, Lord?' And the Lord said to me, 'Arise and go into Damascus, and there you will be told all things which are appointed for you to do.'

Questions:

a. Do you think that it is very difficult to be a committed Christian? Why?

_____

b. In v.10, how did Saul show his commitment to the Lord upon his conversion?

_____

2 Crucial Questions

Receiving Jesus as our Savior from sin brings us into a life-changing relationship with the Son of God. Although we may not know at the time all the far-reaching implications of our commitment to Him, we cannot escape the fact that because He is God, He has a right to be Lord of every area of our lives. Sooner or later we must come to that point where we confess, in the words of Thomas, "My Lord and my God!" (John 20:28).

In Saul's conversion experience, he recognized Jesus as both Savior and Lord. When Saul heard Jesus' voice on the Damascus highway, he asked this crucial question: "Who are You, Lord?" From the answer, "I am Jesus," Paul instantly realized that the One he had been persecuting truly was the Savior. In that moment he cast himself on His mercy. Trembling in God's presence, he asked a second crucial question, "Lord, what do You want me to do?" He was, as Oswald Chambers puts it, "giving up his right to himself."

Believer, you've trusted Jesus as your Savior. You've settled the issue of who He is. But have you asked that second crucial question, "Lord, what do You want me to do?" Say to Him today, "Lord, I'll do whatever You ask!" —DJD

> *Take my life and let it be*
> *Consecrated, Lord, to Thee;*
> *Take my hands and let them move*
> *At the impulse of Thy love.* —Havergal

Because Christ purchased us, He has the right to possess us.

---

c. Are you prepared to trust and obey God in every aspect of your life? Identify one area in which you may find it difficult.

Interesting words:

Way: Here, it means the followers of the Christian religion or simply Christians.

Discovery

19

Read Psalm 95

[1] Oh come, let us sing to the LORD! Let us shout joyfully to the Rock of our salvation. [2] Let us come before His presence with thanksgiving; let us shout joyfully to Him with psalms. [3] For the LORD is the great God, and the great King above all gods. [4] In His hand are the deep places of the earth; the heights of the hills are His also. [5] The sea is His, for He made it; and His hands formed the dry land. [6] Oh come, let us worship and bow down; let us kneel before the LORD our Maker. [7] For He is our God, and we are the people of His pasture, and the sheep of His hand. Today, if you will hear His voice: [8] "Do not harden your hearts, as in the rebellion, as in the day of trial in the wilderness, [9] When your fathers tested Me; they tried Me, though they saw My work. [10] For forty years I was grieved with that generation, and said, 'It is a people who go astray in their hearts, and they do not know My ways.' [11] So I swore in My wrath, 'They shall not enter My rest.'"

Key verse: Psalm 95:6-7

Oh come, let us worship and bow down; let us kneel before the LORD our Maker. For He is our God, and we are the people of His pasture, and the sheep of His hand.

Questions:

a. What are some things you already know about worshipping God?

_____

b. What are some of the characteristics of God that stirred the psalmist to worship Him?

_____

H*i.For*m

My 17-year-old daughter Julie and a co-worker at a department store were meeting for lunch. He had some questions about life, and Julie was glad to talk to him about her faith. As they sat down with their tacos (sandwiches), Julie bowed her head to thank the Lord for her food. When she looked up, her friend said, "I didn't pray. Will God kill me for that?"

His response reveals much about how people view God. Many think our Godward actions —worship—are done as safety devices to prevent the Lord from zapping us. When we think of Him that way, we will have wrong motives for any God-directed action. That kind of thinking leads us to worship God for personal gain or approval.

Our worship of the Lord is not done so we can somehow benefit. Instead, every heavenward thought or action (for example: praying, reading the Bible and obeying) should be done out of honor for Him and His greatness. Our hearts should be filled with the kind of praise expressed in Psalm 95.

Sure, we benefit when we turn our attention to God, but that should not be our motivation. It's not for us that we worship God. It should always be for Him. —JDB

> Then let us adore and give Him His right,
> *All glory and power, all wisdom and might,*
> *All honor and blessing, with angels above,*
> *And thanks never-ceasing for infinite love.* —Wesley

True worship gives God centerstage.

c. To have a better understanding of what true worship is, read "What Kind of Worship is God Looking For?" To order this booklet, please use Order Form on page 61.

Interesting words:

Worship: To prostrate oneself and pay homage before a superior being.
Rock of our salvation: "Rock" is a poetic figure for God, symbolizing His unfailing strength as Deliverer.

Discovery

20

Read 1 Timothy 2:1-8

¹ Therefore I exhort first of all that supplications, prayers, intercessions, and giving of thanks be made for all men, ² for kings and all who are in authority, that we may lead a quiet and peaceable life in all godliness and reverence. ³ For this is good and acceptable in the sight of God our Savior, ⁴ who desires all men to be saved and to come to the knowledge of the truth. ⁵ For there is one God and one Mediator between God and men, the Man Christ Jesus, ⁶ who gave Himself a ransom for all, to be testified in due time, ⁷ for which I was appointed a preacher and an apostle—I am speaking the truth in Christ and not lying—a teacher of the Gentiles in faith and truth. ⁸ I desire therefore that the men pray everywhere, lifting up holy hands, without wrath and doubting.

Praying for Them

Key verse: 1 Timothy 2:1

Therefore I exhort first of all that supplications, prayers, intercessions, and giving of thanks be made for all men.

Questions:

a. Have you ever prayed for someone else to receive Christ?

_____

b. From the passage, why do you think Christians should pray for "all men"?

_____

Prayer Evangelism

Over the centuries since Jesus died for our sins and rose victorious from the grave, many methods have been used to spread the gospel. From Peter's first sermon, when 3,000 were saved, to great preaching campaigns of men like Charles Spurgeon and Billy Sunday, to friendship evangelism, many ways of influencing others to accept Jesus' free gift have been tried.

In a major city in the midwest, another method has been launched: prayer evangelism. In the campaign to reach the populace of this city, organizers have set out to pray for every individual. They have divided the city into sections, and all cooperating churches have been assigned the names of the people in those sections.

Of course, it will also take other kinds of essential contacts, such as literature or face-to-face visits, but prayer is the major component. In 1 Timothy, Paul explained that God "desires all men to be saved and to come to the knowledge of the truth" (1 Timothy 2:4). And the method suggested for beginning the work of evangelization is "supplications, prayers, intercessions . . . for all men" (v. 1).

What about your neighborhood and mine? Let's begin right now to pray for people individually. —JDB

> A burden for souls, dear Lord,
> A burden to share.
> A love for the lost, dear Lord,
> A genuine care. —Anon.

Talk to God about people before you talk to people about God.

---

c. List the names of five people (your friends or your family) who have not received Christ. Pray for them individually. Ask God to give you an opportunity to talk to them about the Gospel.

Interesting words:

Exhort: Encourage, challenge.
Supplications: Requests.
Intercessions: Prayers on behalf of a person or group.
Godliness: An attitude of reverence, devotion and a life of obedience toward God.

Discovery

21

Read Hebrews 10:19-25

¹⁹ Therefore, brethren, having boldness to enter the Holiest by the blood of Jesus, ²⁰ by a new and living way which He consecrated for us, through the veil, that is, His flesh, ²¹ and having a High Priest over the house of God, ²² let us draw near with a true heart in full assurance of faith, having our hearts sprinkled from an evil conscience and our bodies washed with pure water. ²³ Let us hold fast the confession of our hope without wavering, for He who promised is faithful. ²⁴ And let us consider one another in order to stir up love and good works, ²⁵ not forsaking the assembling of ourselves together, as is the manner of some, but exhorting one another, and so much the more as you see the Day approaching.

Key verse: Hebrews 10:24-25

And let us consider one another in order to stir up love and good works, not forsaking the assembling of ourselves together, as is the manner of some, but exhorting one another, and so much the more as you see the Day approaching.

Questions:

a. Think about something loving and good that someone has recently done for you.

_____

b. From Hebrews 10:24-25, what are two things we should do to stir up love and good works among Christians?

_____

Grasshopper Christians

One grasshopper seems insignificant as it leaps across the lawn. But when it joins forces with other grasshoppers, the resulting swarm can soon devour all the vegetation in its path.

Grasshoppers demonstrate the power of community. What they cannot do by themselves, they can accomplish together. In the book of Proverbs, the wise man Agur observed, "The locusts have no king, yet they all advance in ranks" (Proverbs 30:27).

We can learn a lesson from these little creatures. Believers can make far greater advances for Christ's cause when they act and pray together than they could ever make alone. When Christians are united in serving the Lord, they can become a mighty force for God.

Although the New Testament urges us to possess a personal faith in Jesus Christ, it says nothing at all about a private faith. We need other believers, and other believers need us.

Let's enjoy the strength and fellowship available in the unified body of Christ. An effective church will reflect "the good sense of the grasshopper" by its love and unity in the Holy Spirit. —HWR

We all depend upon the strength
We draw from one another,
For we are one in faith and love
With every Christian brother. —Sper

Two Christians are better than one—when they're one.

---

c. What are some ways you can do to help a Christian friend do what is pleasing to God?

_____

Interesting words:

Holiest: Here, it means the very Presence of God.

Stir up: Encouragement to some action or feeling.

Day: The Second Coming of Christ.

Discovery

22

Read Psalm 139:1-10

¹O LORD, You have searched me and known me. ²You know my sitting down and my rising up; you understand my thought afar off. ³You comprehend my path and my lying down, and are acquainted with all my ways. ⁴For there is not a word on my tongue, but behold, O LORD, You know it altogether. ⁵You have hedged me behind and before, and laid Your hand upon me. ⁶Such knowledge is too wonderful for me; it is high, I cannot attain it. ⁷Where can I go from Your Spirit? Or where can I flee from Your presence? ⁸If I ascend into heaven, You are there; if I make my bed in hell, behold, You are there. ⁹If I take the wings of the morning, and dwell in the uttermost parts of the sea, ¹⁰ even there Your hand shall lead me, and Your right hand shall hold me.

Key verse: Psalm 139:7-8

Where can I go from Your Spirit? Or where can I flee from Your presence?

Questions:

a. Do you sometimes feel that God is far away? How does it feel then to know that God knows everything about you?

_____

b. From vv.2-4, what are some things the writer says God knows about you?

_____

a *From Distance*

A few years ago, a popular song was Bette Midler's 'From A Distance.' Its call for world unity received much response during the Persian Gulf conflict. I don't know the spiritual background of Julia Gold, the song's composer, but she did have her theology straight in one sense. As the song's chorus reminded us, "God is watching us, from a distance." The song is right. According to 2 Chronicles 16:9, "The eyes of the Lord range throughout the earth."

An astronaut who has seen our world 'from a distance' describes the view in pretty striking terms. According to Jack Lousma, he and his fellow astronauts could see man-made freeways and airports, as well as natural wonders such as rivers and deserts.

Some view! Of course, God has a better view than anybody does, astronauts included. But His view is even more detailed. He can see each of us individually—He even knows our thoughts! The idea of being under God's constant gaze shouldn't bother us, however. It's just another way that He demonstrates His faithful love and care for us.

True, if we are harboring sin, the guilt could make God's watchfulness a little disturbing, as it did for Adam and Eve (Genesis 3:8-10). But for those who enjoy a close, intimate relationship with Him, God's global viewpoint is comforting. This may sound kind of scary, but God is watching you right now. Why not thank Him that He can see everything that happens to you—and that He cares so deeply for you! —JC

God is always present with us,
Though His face we cannot see;
He protects and guides and comforts
All His children faithfully. —Sper

God's presence with us is His greatest present to us.

---

c. How will knowing that God "watches" over you every moment of your life affect the way you think, talk and act?

Interesting words:

Hedged: Here, it means surrounded or put under scrutiny.

Discovery
23

Read 1 Thessalonians 5:16-18

¹⁶ Rejoice always, ¹⁷ pray without ceasing, ¹⁸ in everything give thanks; for this is the will of God in Christ Jesus for you.

Key verse: 1 Thessalonians 5:18

In everything give thanks; for this is the will of God in Christ Jesus for you.

Questions:

a. Do you find it difficult to thank another person for some good done to you?

_____

b. What does Paul mean when he tells us to "give thanks in everything"?

_____

Count your blessings

Missionary Benjamin Weir was held hostage in Lebanon and imprisoned under miserable conditions for 16 months. In his first interview after his release, he was asked how he spent his time and how he dealt with boredom and despair. His answer stunned the reporters. He simply said, "Counting my blessings."

"Blessings?" they responded.

"Yes," he explained. "Some days I got to take a shower. Sometimes there were some vegetables in my food. And I could always be thankful for the love of my family."

We can understand why the reporters were astonished. It's hard for most of us to be consistently thankful for the commonplace blessings that make life pleasant and comfortable —the unfailing supply of our daily needs, the provision of food and shelter, the companionship of friends and family. There are times when we may even forget the wonderful mercies of God's redeeming grace.

Paul and Silas, though they were beaten, thrown into prison, and placed in stocks, were still 'singing hymns to God' (Acts 16:25). May we learn from them, and from Benjamin Weir, to count our blessings no matter what our circumstances. We have many reasons to rejoice. —VCG

> We should be ready to give the Lord thanks
> *For blessing as well as for test;*
> *Hearts that are thankful is all that He asks;*
> *Let's trust Him to give what is best.* —Bierema

If you pause to think, you'll have cause to thank.

c. What are some things you can thank God for?

_____

Interesting words:

Pray without ceasing: To pray every time an opportunity presents itself and to be in constant attitude of dependence on God.
Will of God: What God wants us to do.

Discovery
24

Read Mark 10:35-45

[35] Then James and John, the sons of Zebedee, came to Him, saying, "Teacher, we want You to do for us whatever we ask." [36] And He said to them, "What do you want Me to do for you?" [37] They said to Him, "Grant us that we may sit, one on Your right hand and the other on Your left, in Your glory." [38] But Jesus said to them, "You do not know what you ask. Can you drink the cup that I drink, and be baptized with the baptism that I am baptized with?" [39] They said to Him, "We are able." So Jesus said to them, "You will indeed drink the cup that I drink, and with the baptism I am baptized with you will be baptized; [40] but to sit on My right hand and on My left is not Mine to give, but it is for those for whom it is prepared." [41] And when the ten heard it, they began to be greatly displeased with James and John. [42] But Jesus called them to Himself and said to them, "You know that those who are considered rulers over the Gentiles lord it over them, and their great ones exercise authority over them. [43] Yet it shall not be so among you; but whoever desires to become great among you shall be your servant. [44] And whoever of you desires to be first shall be slave of all. [45] For even the Son of Man did not come to be served, but to serve, and to give His life a ransom for many."

Key verse: Mark 10:43-44

Yet it shall not be so among you; but whoever desires to become great among you shall be your servant. And whoever of you desires to be first shall be slave of all.

Questions:

a. Why do you think some people want to be leaders?

b. What is the difference between being great in this world (v.42) and being great in God's Kingdom (vv.43-44)?

King of the Apes

Studies conducted by the National Geographic Society provide some fascinating insights into the behavior of chimpanzees. Observers noted how the leadership of a chimp community changed because of a dramatic bluff used by one of the lowliest members of the colony.

Mike, as he was affectionately known, learned to dominate his chimp establishment with the aid of some empty kerosene cans and a heavy steel box. Hooting loudly, he would bang the metal objects together as he pushed them over the ground. This clamorous behavior frightened the apes so much that the leader surrendered his sovereignty to Mike.

Unfortunately, similar situations may be seen in the church. Those who generate the most activity often receive the greatest attention and honor. But a big program and a flashy personality are not sure evidence of divine blessing.

Paul warned against looking at things according to the outward appearance (2 Corinthians 10:7). The real measure of our labor is whether it is in keeping with God's Word and reflects His glory rather than our own.

Make sure that whatever you do, you do for the Lord. Then when you glory, it will be in Him! —MRDII

> Help us not to cloud God's glory,
> Nor with self His light to dim;
> May each thought to Christ be captive,
> Emptied to be filled with Him. —Anon.

You can't glorify self and Christ at the same time.

---

c. In our service to God, we tend to allow recognition and praise to become our primary motivation. Pray and ask God to help you be motivated only by a desire to be His servant.

Interesting words:

Baptized: Here, it means being identified with Christ's death and resurrection.

Topic:
KNOWING GOD

Subtopic:
Holy Spirit's Power

Discovery
25

Read John 16:7-15

⁷Nevertheless I tell you the truth. It is to your advantage that I go away; for if I do not go away, the Helper will not come to you; but if I depart, I will send Him to you. ⁸And when He has come, He will convict the world of sin, and of righteousness, and of judgment: ⁹ of sin, because they do not believe in Me; ¹⁰ of righteousness, because I go to My Father and you see Me no more; ¹¹ of judgment, because the ruler of this world is judged. ¹² I still have many things to say to you, but you cannot bear them now. ¹³ However, when He, the Spirit of truth, has come, He will guide you into all truth; for He will not speak on His own authority, but whatever He hears He will speak; and He will tell you things to come. ¹⁴ He will glorify Me, for He will take of what is Mine and declare it to you. ¹⁵ All things that the Father has are Mine. Therefore I said that He will take of Mine and declare it to you.

Key verse: John 13-14

However, when He, the Spirit of truth, has come, He will guide you into all truth; for He will not speak on His own authority, but whatever He hears He will speak; and He will tell you things to come. He will glorify Me, for He will take of what is Mine and declare it to you.

Questions:

a. What are some things you already know about the Holy Spirit?

_____

b. According to vv.8 and 13-15, what is the role of the Holy Spirit in relation to us?

_____

Lesson of the 18-Wheeler

I was talking with a veteran truck driver about his life on the road. We discussed interstates, cities, truck stops, engines, and tractors. As he spoke about his huge rig, he referred several times to steering axles and drive axles. I asked him to explain the difference. He told me that the front axle of a truck is the steering axle. The drive axles, located under the rear of the cab, transfer the power that is generated by the diesel engine. It's the drive axles that enable the semi to climb steep grades, inch down dangerous slopes, and barrel down the highway to get the load in on time.

My discussion with that trucker gave me a new appreciation for those 18-wheelers, and it reminded me of a spiritual truth. Just as steering axles and drive axles are essential to a tractor-trailer, so also direction and power are vital to followers of Christ as we travel through life. The Holy Spirit provides us with both. He was sent to guide us into all truth (John 16:13) and to teach us (1 Corinthians 2:10-16). We are empowered by the Spirit to witness (Acts 1:8), to pray (Romans 8:26), and to live a hope-filled life (Romans 15:13).

The next time one of those big semis blows by you on the highway, think about the lesson of the 18-wheeler. Depend on the Holy Spirit for direction and strength. —DCE

The Spirit gives us power to live
A life that's pleasing to the Lord;
He also guides us and provides
Direction in God's holy Word. —Sper

The power that drives us comes from the Spirit inside us.

c. To have a better understanding of who the Holy Spirit is and His role in the life of the Christian, read "The Promise of the Holy Spirit". To order this booklet, please use Order Form on page 61.

Interesting words:

Helper: Comforter, Counsellor, someone who comes alongside and helps another in trouble.
Righteousness: Holy living that meets God's standard.
Glorify: To magnify or ascribe honour.

Discovery

26

Read 1 Samuel 15:1-3, 7-11

¹ Samuel also said to Saul, "The LORD sent me to anoint you king over His people, over Israel. Now therefore, heed the voice of the words of the LORD. ² Thus says the LORD of hosts: 'I will punish Amalek for what he did to Israel, how he ambushed him on the way when he came up from Egypt. ³ Now go and attack Amalek, and utterly destroy all that they have, and do not spare them. . . ' "

⁷And Saul attacked the Amalekites, from Havilah all the way to Shur, which is east of Egypt. ⁸ He also took Agag king of the Amalekites alive, and utterly destroyed all the people with the edge of the sword. ⁹ But Saul and the people spared Agag and the best of the sheep, the oxen, the fatlings, the lambs, and all that was good, and were unwilling to utterly destroy them. . .¹⁰ Now the word of the LORD came to Samuel, saying, ¹¹ "I greatly regret that I have set up Saul as king, for he has turned back from following Me, and has not performed My commandments."

Obedience

Key verse: 1 Samuel 15:11

"I greatly regret that I have set up Saul as king, for he has turned back from following Me, and has not performed My commandments. . . "

Questions:

a. Are there times when you find it difficult to obey God? Write down what you thought and did in one such instance.

_____

b. Why did Saul not obey God completely (vv.9-10)?

_____

100% Obedience

As the father of an elementary-school-age boy, I think I know why God places so much emphasis on obedience. Boys can get themselves into so much difficulty so easily. I can't imagine the trouble they would get into if they weren't required to obey anyone.

Take, for instance, my rule about crossing the street. Steven knows that he's supposed to stop at the end of the driveway and look both ways—whether he is riding his bike, roller blading, or just chasing a ball. I expect 100-percent obedience because I know that it takes only one careless step into the street to jeopardize his safety. Steven may not know why I have set the rule, but he trusts that I love him and rules are for his own good.

When God sent Saul to attack the Amalekites, he commanded Saul to destroy everything that belonged to them. Saul did not obey God totally. He spared Agag and everything that was good. Saul probably did not see the reason why God wanted him to destroy everything. Instead of trusting God, he disobeyed God, and he had to face the consequences. The Lord, who is a perfect Father, loves us and knows what will work out best in our lives. To show that we trust Him, we need to do all we can to obey what He has told us in the Bible, His Word. He deserves our 100-percent obedience. —JDB

Let your days be Mine to order;
Where I lead, obedient be.
Let your own desires be nothing;
Only seek to follow Me. —Anon.

The cost of obedience is nothing compared to the cost of disobedience.

c. Is there an area in your life where you have not obeyed God fully? Do so now.

Interesting words:

Amalekites: People of ancient times that were Israel's enemies.

Discovery
27

Read 1 Thessalonians 1:5-8

⁵ For our gospel did not come to you in word only, but also in power, and in the Holy Spirit and in much assurance, as you know what kind of men we were among you for your sake. ⁶ And you became followers of us and of the Lord, having received the word in much affliction, with joy of the Holy Spirit, ⁷ so that you became examples to all in Macedonia and Achaia who believe. ⁸ For from you the word of the Lord has sounded forth, not only in Macedonia and Achaia, but also in every place. Your faith toward God has gone out, so that we do not need to say anything.

Key verse: 1 Thessalonians 1:8

For from you the word of the Lord has sounded forth, not only in Macedonia and Achaia, but also in every place. Your faith toward God has gone out, so that we do not need to say anything.

Questions:

a. How do you think we should respond to the command God has given us to tell others about Jesus?

_____

b. How did the Macedonians and Achaians come to know about Jesus through the Thessalonians (vv.6-8)?

_____

How will they Hear?

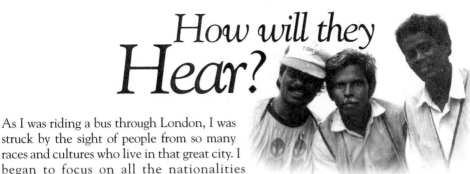

As I was riding a bus through London, I was struck by the sight of people from so many races and cultures who live in that great city. I began to focus on all the nationalities represented and wondered how the whole world would ever hear the gospel of Jesus Christ.

While I was deep in thought, a woman stopped next to my seat. With a beautiful smile, she extended a sheet of paper and asked, "Would you like to read about being born again?" I thanked her and told her that I knew the Lord Jesus Christ. "Praise God," she said quietly, and moved on to the next person.

I thought, that's how they'll hear! One at a time they'll hear the gospel from faithful believers who reach out to others wherever they are. The woman on the bus made me think of Paul's commendation to the Christians in Thessalonica: "From you the word of the Lord has sounded forth, not only in Macedonia and Achaia, but also in every place" (1 Thessalonians 1:8). Instead of being paralyzed by the thought that millions haven't heard, she was sharing Christ with a few, right where she lived. What if we all did that—starting today?

How will they hear? Only as we reach out to one person at a time and share the saving gospel of Jesus Christ. —DCM

We know that millions haven't heard
About God's only Son,
So we must witness where we are
And tell them one by one. —Sper

Reach out to a world in need with the Word it needs.

---

c. Remember the list of five people (see page 43) that you have been praying for? Ask God to give you the courage and opportunity to share the Gospel with them this week.

Interesting words:

Gospel: The Good News that Christ died for our sins and rose again the third day to give us new life.

Affliction: Here, it means difficulties and persecution.

Discovery

28

Read Philippians 2:1-11

[1] Therefore if there is any consolation in Christ, if any comfort of love, if any fellowship of the Spirit, if any affection and mercy, [2] fulfil my joy by being like-minded, having the same love, being of one accord, of one mind. [3] Let nothing be done through selfish ambition or conceit, but in lowliness of mind let each esteem others better than himself. [4] Let each of you look out not only for his own interests, but also for the interests of others. [5] Let this mind be in you which was also in Christ Jesus, [6] who, being in the form of God, did not consider it robbery to be equal with God, [7] but made Himself of no reputation, taking the form of a bondservant, and coming in the likeness of men. [8] And being found in appearance as a man, He humbled Himself and became obedient to the point of death, even the death of the cross. [9] Therefore God also has highly exalted Him and given Him the name which is above every name, [10] that at the name of Jesus every knee should bow, of those in heaven, and of those on earth, and of those under the earth, [11] and that every tongue should confess that Jesus Christ is Lord, to the glory of God the Father.

Church in Unity

Key verse: Philippians 2:4

Let each of you look out not only for his own interests, but also for the interests of others.

Questions:

a. What is your first reaction to someone who offends you?

b. What does the passage tell us about the way we should look at and relate with others?

Others *or* Me?

When Paul wrote the letter to the church of Philippi, he wanted to encourage them not to have disunity in church. This disunity comes when some members of the church put self above others. However, that's not an example Christ shows us. In fact, when on the cross Jesus took the penalty we deserved, He put the welfare of others ahead of His own.

O, that we would follow His example in our churches, and realize that the church is bigger than any individual, its ministry far more important than our personal rights and desires! If we would only ask, "How would my action affect the church and what Christ wants us to do?" Instead, we insist on our rights and hold to our position, even though it splits the church, ruins our testimony (our example as a Christian), and stops progress.

One summer I was picking beans near one of my beehives. Some of the bees spotted me and supposed me to be the enemy. In their attack, two bees stung me and died in the defense of the hive. They had only one goal—the safety of the others in the hive, so they gave their lives for the good of the many.

Instead of being angry, I admired those bees and prayed that we would be like that: not seeking our own comfort and safety, but living for the good of the body of Christ! —MRD

> *All of us chose to be a sinner,*
> *All we deserve is death forever.*
> *All to save us Christ has suffered,*
> *Although we don't deserve what He has offered.*
> *And so, my brothers, allow me to be*
> *As Christ, in His grace, has been to me.*
> *All my rights I give willingly*
> *All to serve and suffer for thee. —LLS*

Consider others before self.

c. Identify a person that you find difficult to accept. In the light of this study, pray for a change in your attitude towards him/her.

Interesting words:

Consolation: Encouragement.
Being of one accord, of one mind: Signifies community of love and unity.
Lowliness of mind: Humble, correct estimate of oneself
Esteem: Consider respectfully.

Congratulations! You made it!

Now that you've completed all 28 discoveries, has it given you a thirst for a deeper relationship with God?

Before you head out for the high seas, here's a thought for you. Someone said that God's Word is simple enough for a babe to wade in and deep enough for philosophers to drown in. Yes, God's Word isn't something you can plumb just by having a short swim in it once in a while when you feel like it. It's serious business! That shouldn't discourage you, however.

Just remember, the most important thing about studying the Bible is letting it change our lives. So don't stop hungering and thirsting after God's Word: what God does in your life through it will be of lasting value!

You may not have noticed, but along the way, these studies have been equipping you to study the Bible for yourself. We weren't kidding when we said that walking with God was a lifelong adventure! So venture out courageously to study God's Word for yourself. Never fear! There will be people, books and materials to help you along the way.

Bon voyage, my friend!

For Your Further Reading And Study

If you would like to have some of these booklets, please check the relevant boxes and mail this form to the RBC Ministries office. We will endeavor to mail you the available booklets. Please note that your request is subject to the availability of booklets at the time of processing.

☐	Can Anyone Really Know For Sure?	Q0601
☐	How Can I Resist The Lure Of Sexual Sin?	Q0707
☐	How Can I Break The Silence?	Q0706
☐	Why Would A Good God Allow Suffering?	Q0106
☐	What Kind Of Worship Is God Looking For?	Q0902
☐	The Promise Of The Holy Spirit	Q0306

Please print clearly in block letters:

Name :_____

Address :_____

_____Postal Code :_____

City :_____ Country :_____

Home Tel :_____Office Tel :_____ Fax :_____

E-Mail :_____Church :_____

Support for RBC Ministries comes from the gifts of our members and friends.

Please send to:

**Radio Bible Class
PO Box 1
Carnforth, Lancs, LA5 9ES,
England**

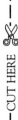

CUT HERE

Our Daily Bread

D e l i v e r e d   t o   Y o u r   H o m e !

You can begin to receive *Our Daily Bread* at your home or your office. Just mail us this request form today! We'd love to welcome you as a regular member of RBC Ministries.

Once you are a member, you will receive:

Our Daily Bread: Daily devotional articles that will challenge and inspire you as you spend time in God's Word.

Discovery Series: Bible study booklets providing insight to a variety of subjects for people eager to apply God's Word to their lives. We will send you one title with *Our Daily Bread* each quarter.

☐ **Yes!** I want to become a member of RBC Ministries and receive *Our Daily Bread* regularly.

Send me: (Quarterly) ☐ English ODB ☐ Spanish ODB ☐ Portuguese ODB

Please do not complete this form if you are already receiving Our Daily Bread from us each quarter.

Please print clearly in block letters:

Name :_____

Address :_____

_____Postal Code :_____

City :_____ Country :_____

Home Tel :_____Office Tel :_____ Fax :_____

E-Mail :_____Church :_____

Support for RBC Ministries comes from the gifts of our members and friends.

✂ CUT HERE

Reflections

Reflections

Printed by Printcorp. LP № 347 of 11.05.99. Kuprevich St. 18, Minsk, 220141.
Ord. 0248. Qty 30 000 cps.